Paul Strathern was born in London and studied philosophy at Trinity College, Dublin. He was a lecturer at Kingston University where he taught philosophy and mathematics. He is a Somerset Maugham prize-winning novelist. He is also the author of the *Philosophers in 90 Minutes* series. He wrote *Mendeleyev's Dream* which was shortlisted for the Aventis Science Book Prize, *Dr. Strangelove's Game: A History of Economic Genius, The Medici: Godfathers of the Renaissance, Napoleon in Egypt* and most recently, *The Artist, The Philosopher and The Warrior*, which details the convergence of three of Renaissance Italy's most brilliant minds: Leonardo Da Vinci, Niccolo Machiavelli and Cesare Borgia. He lives in London and has three grandchildren.

In THE BIG IDEA series:

GALILEO & THE SOLAR SYSTEM

The Big Idea

PAUL STRATHERN

arrow books

Reissued by Arrow Books 2009

3 5 7 9 10 8 6 4 2

First published in Great Britain in 1998 by Arrow Books

The Random House Group Limited
20 Vauxhall Bridge Road, London SW1V 2SA

www.rbooks.co.uk

Addresses for companies within The Random House Group Limited
can be found at: www.randomhouse.co.uk/offices.htm

The Random House Group Limited Reg. No. 954009

A CIP catalogue record for this book
is available from the British Library

ISBN 9780099238027

The Random House Group Limited supports The Forest Stewardship
Council (FSC), the leading international forest certification organisation.
All our titles that are printed on Greenpeace approved FSC certified paper
carry the FSC logo. Our paper procurement policy can be found at
www.rbooks.co.uk/environment.

Mixed Sources
Product group from well-managed
forests and other controlled sources
www.fsc.org Cert no. TT-COC-2139
© 1996 Forest Stewardship Council

Typeset in Bembo by SX Composing DTP, Rayleigh, Essex
Printed and bound in the United Kingdom by
CPI Cox & Wyman, Reading, RG1 8EX

CONTENTS

INTRODUCTION

Galileo could have become the first (and last) great scientific martyr. But he wisely shirked this role. Instead, he chose to swear that he'd got it all wrong – whilst remaining well aware that swearing had nothing to do with it.

Galileo spans the age between the Renaissance of Leonardo and the Scientific Age of Newton. The Renaissance saw the rebirth of the ancient Greek ideas of truth – truth shown by investigation or proof, rather than reference to authority. The resulting self-confident humanism inspired speculation over the entire field of learning. But most of this was like Leonardo's notebooks – wide-ranging, brilliant, but unsystematic and lacking any underlying principle. Such were the thinkers who broke the ice in the long scientific ice age of the Medieval era.

After Leonardo came the age of Descartes

and Galileo. The French philosopher Descartes introduced the philosophy of reason, based upon his celebrated premise 'I think therefore I am'. Galileo gave eyes and senses to this newborn reason. The thermometer, various measuring devices, a vastly improved telescope – with these Galileo confirmed the scientific nature of reality and the Sun's place at the centre of the solar system. Previously it had been thought that the laws of physics applied only on Earth. The planets and the stars worked according to a heavenly system of their own.

After Galileo, the way was left open for an all-embracing scientific explanation of the universe. In the ensuing age, Newton came up with the first answer to this question. It remains the Big Question, and continues to obsess science today.

LIFE & WORKS

Galileo Galilei was born in Pisa on 15th February 1564 – just three days before the death of the 89-year-old Michelangelo, last of the heroes of the high Renaissance. Galileo's family is said to have originated from the Mugello, a remote valley 15 miles north across the mountains from Florence. This tiny isolated region must have had a remarkable gene pool, for it also produced the artists Fra Angelico and Giotto, and the Medici family.

Galileo's father, Vincenzo, was descended from a noble Florentine family of dwindling fortune. He had little money, and a combative temperament which ensured that he remained in this situation. But he was also a man of genuine talent, who had studied music in Venice and had become a leading expert in musical theory. He rebelled against the strait-jacket of counterpoint – insisting that music should please the ear in practice, rather than the mind in formal theory on the page. His written works played their part in the freeing of music which was to result in the birth of opera by the end of the century.

Like father, like son. Galileo grew into a bright and bumptious red-headed lad, whose obvious extrovert charms concealed a rather more complex temperament. Life at home was not easy. His mother, Giulia, considered that she had married beneath her. Being married to a ne'er-do-well, as she saw it, soon embittered her. She became a nagging wife and a demanding mother. Galileo became used to being the centre of his mother's attention, and benefitted from the self-confidence this inspired – but beneath his ebullience there always lurked the uncertainties bred of his stormy home life.

When Galileo was ten the family moved to Florence, where his father became a court musician and well-known controversialist. For his education, the young Galileo was sent to the monastery at Vallombrosa in the mountains 15 miles east of the city. Here he was so taken by the monastic life that he chose to become a novice. But Vincenzo had other ideas for his son, and at 14 he was removed from Vallombrosa and sent to tutors in Florence.

In 1581, at the age of 17, Galileo went back to his home town, to study medicine at the University of Pisa. His father wanted him to become a doctor, so he could bring in some much-needed cash for the family.

In Pisa, Galileo quickly became bored with the curriculum of medieval scholasticism. Outside the university a new age had begun. The Renaissance had transformed art and architecture, introducing a new era of self-confidence. Commerce and banking were revitalizing Europe. Luther and Calvin had broken the hegemony of the Church. Columbus had opened up the Americas and the Portugese were trading with China. But still education remained traditional and unchanged. Aristotle's outmoded natural philosophy continued to rule supreme; medicine was still rooted in Galen's dangerously inadequate physiology; and the interpretation of Latin and Greek texts remained the order of the day.

Galileo made no secret of his contempt for his lecturers. They were frequently wrong, and he insisted upon exposing them as such. He would stand up in lectures and pose ironic questions. According to Aristotle, heavier bodies fell faster than lighter ones – so how come all hailstones hit the ground at the same speed? The lecturer explained that the lighter hailstones obviously fell from a lower part of the sky. Galileo treated such explanations with the contempt they deserved, and his arrogance was treated with an equally well-deserved contempt by the authorities. Galileo may have had intellectual acumen, but he was decidedly lacking in social acumen. He even patronized his fellow students. Galileo was too bright for his own good, and in the absence of any intellectual challenge he sought stimulus elsewhere in the taverns and bordellos.

Roistering came naturally to the lively red-bearded student, but he had an even more avaricious intellectual appetite. Things always livened up between Christmas and Easter when the Grand Duke of Tuscany moved his court from Florence to Pisa. For a few months the provincial backwater became a social hub, with all kinds of cosmopolitan entertainment. Galileo managed to sneak into a private lecture given by the court mathematician Ostilio Ricci, and was at once enthralled. He had always been attracted by abstract calculation, but the university considered mathematics as largely irrelevant. (After the professor of mathematics at Pisa passed on, the chair of mathematics remained unfilled through the years when Galileo was there.)

Galileo made a habit of sneaking into Ricci's lectures, which were intended for the young men of the court. Emboldened, the student gatecrasher approached Ricci and began asking him questions after his lectures. Ricci quickly realised that Galileo had exceptional talents, and encouraged him.

Galileo had at last found a teacher he could admire. Ricci was no ordinary court mathematician, he was also an exceptional military engineer. (Some years later he would be commissioned to reconstruct the island fortress of the Château d'If off Marseilles, whose fortifications feature in Alexandre Dumas' famous yarn *The Count of Monte Cristo*.) Ricci showed that there was money to be made out of mathematics, when it was put to practical use.

Vincenzo was not happy when he heard of his son's neglect of his medical studies. But he was already beginning to accept that his son would never be a doctor: he just didn't have the temperament. When the court returned to Florence, Vincenzo approached Ricci and asked if he would give Galileo lessons. Ricci began instructing Galileo in Euclid and Archimedes. Euclid's clarity and rigour of argument were a revelation to Galileo. Traditional scholastic argument appealed to established authorities such as Aristotle. Euclid's authority was truth, only this was considered sufficient to prove his arguments. In his *Elements* Euclid laid down the foundations of geometry, and outlined the method to be adopted by mathematics. Starting from the simplest self-evident definitions (for a point, a line, and so forth), he then proceeded to theorems, each of which was rigidly proved, one following on from the other, building up the irrefutable structure of geometry.

After Euclid came Archimedes, who had died in 212 BC. Galileo recognized at once the quality of the ancient Greek's expertise: 'Those who read his works realise only too clearly how inferior all other minds are.' He was the greatest mathematician of all time. But here was more than just theoretical brilliance. Besides advancing numerology and calculating the properties of parabolic solids,

Archimedes had also pioneered statics, single-handedly founded hydrostatics, produced pulleys and even invented a water pump.

Galileo soon demonstrated that he too was exceptionally gifted in the practical sphere. According to a much recounted story, one Sunday when he was sitting through a long sermon in Pisa cathedral, he became intrigued by a swinging lamp hanging on a long wire from the ceiling. He noticed that no matter how wide the arc of its swing, the lamp took precisely the same time to complete one oscillation. In a flash of inspiration, Galileo realized that it was just like a pulse. As soon as he returned home he constructed a pendulum with a piece of string and a lead weight. He then conducted a number of experiments, with differing weights and differing lengths of string. On the strength of these experiments he constructed a pendulum device which could be used for timing a patient's pulse. This he showed to some faculty members of the university medical department, who were so impressed that they immediately pinched his idea. Despite this the *pulsilogium*, as it came to be called, brought Galileo a certain amount of local renown. But when examples of this device went into use in cities throughout Italy, he received neither cash nor credit for his invention. (The concept of patent law was entirely foreign to 16th century Italy, where secrecy, plagiarism, spying and fakery were all considered part of the manufacturing process.)

As a result of such commercial practice, and other practices which Galileo indulged in the taverns, he eventually ran out of cash. In 1685, after four years at university, he returned home to Florence without a degree. But such lack of qualifications was not sufficient to discourage a self-confident character like Galileo. He immediately set up as a mathematician, delivering lectures on this subject where and when he could. At first takers were understandably scarce, and he even had to resort to some teaching at his old school in Vallombrosa.

Eventually Vincenzo managed to pull a few strings at court, and Galileo secured some occasional lecturing at the prestigous Florentine Academy. This had been founded in the 1660s by the first Medici Grand Duke of Tuscany, Cosimo I, (not to be confused with the great banker and patron Cosimo pater patriae, the founder of the

Medici dynasty, who ruled the city during the early Renaissance in the previous century). The Florentine Academy continued to uphold the noblest ideals of the Renaissance. It aimed to produce the 'universal man', whose knowledge extended throughout the entire sphere of learning, a breadth complemented by the depth of his wisdom.

By 1585, Cosimo I had been succeeded by his son Francesco I, who was particularly interested in the new sciences. He even had his own private laboratory in the Medici Palace, where he is said to have undertaken the first successful experiment to melt rock crystals. Unfortunately this breadth of scientific expertise was only matched by the breadth of his gullibility. Francesco I was a great believer in quack medicines, which in the best scientific tradition he insisted upon trying out on himself. He was to die in 1687 after attempting to cure himself of a fever with a remedy which, according to Galileo's biographer James Reston, 'was extracted from the ducts of the crocodile and mixed with secretions from the porcupine, the Peruvian goat, and the Indian gazelle'. His demise was predictably long and painful.

Galileo's ageing father was meanwhile continuing with his controversies over musical theory. Vincenzo began some experiments aimed at disproving the medieval mathematical theory of harmony. For these he enlisted the help of his son, and together they undertook a series of tests involving stringed instruments. These were intended to show that consonance was not merely controlled by the numerical lengths of the strings. These experiments, and his father's methodology, had a profound effect on Galileo. They taught him the necessity for testing mathematical rules with physical observation. Here the proofs he had so admired in Euclid were transferred to practice.

Galileo's admiration for the ancients remained undimmed, but he was not one to be overawed. Around this time he published a brief work called *La Balancietta*. In this he described Archimedes' famous hydrostatic experiment to detect the amounts of gold and silver used in the making of King Hieron's gold crown (which, according to the fraudulent goldsmith, consisted entirely of gold). Galileo then had the audacity to improve on Archimedes' experiment, describing a much better method of determining the proportions of the different metals — with a hydrostatic scale of his own invention. This scale, known as *la balancietta* (little balance), was an extremely delicate instrument involving the highest technical expertise, and was capable of detecting very small differences in weight. Characteristic both of its age and its inventor, this device was also extremely beautiful. Like his earlier *pulsilogium*, it too became a source of great wonder throughout Italy, but once again Galileo's reward was passing fame rather than fortune. (Though already it was becoming obvious that he had just as much need of glory as he had of gold.)

By now Galileo had realized that his only way to financial security was to win an appointment as professor of mathematics at a university (an unusual aim for someone who had failed his degree). Unfortunately, such posts were few and far between — mathematics was still scorned by Aristotelian academia, regarded as little better than an adjunct to astrology.

Even the Florentine Academy retained a curiously medieval approach to learning. The big question of the day, in Galileo's time, concerned the whereabouts and size of Dante's Inferno. This purely poetic underworld is described in some detail by Dante, including imaginative hints as to its location and proportions. These were taken literally, rather than literarily, by the Academy – but unfortunately the literature department didn't know enough geography or mathematics to come up with any answers. So the question was thrown open to all faculties.

Ever one to leap into the fray, Galileo announced that he would deliver a public lecture in which he would reveal the precise dimensions and geographic location of the elusive Inferno. Many have regarded this as merely another attempt by Galileo to draw attention to himself – a chance to shine in front of the Grand Duke and perhaps gain a powerful patron. But this was not the whole story. Galileo actually believed that Dante's Inferno existed.

In many respects Galileo was to remain a medieval man. His belief in medieval thinking, the authority of the Church, and even literary fairy tales, remained unshaken by his growing scientific awareness. His contempt for authority was restricted to the one field where he knew what he was talking about – and knew that his opponents knew no such thing. In his mind, the medieval and the modern coexisted. Indeed, this conflict between two worlds which didn't fit together may well have provided creative stimulus. (Galileo's contemporary Shakespeare had a similarly divided mind, and an even more schizoid attitude is evident in Galileo's successor Newton, who managed the supreme intellectual feat of believing firmly in both the mathematical universe of astronomy and the magical universe of alchemy.)

Galileo's speech to the Florentine Academy in the hall of the Medici palace in 1588 is indicative of his self-contradictory world view. The authority of the medieval mind of Dante is accepted without question – yet his text is scrutinized with the enquiring mind of the new scientist. Accordingly, Galileo calculated that the Inferno was shaped like an inverted cone and occupied $\frac{1}{12}$ of the Earth's volume below the surface at Jerusalem. For good measure, he even outlined a rigorously mathematical calculation of the size of Lucifer, based entirely upon evidence in Dante's poem. ('. . .we can thus conclude that Lucifer had a height of 1,935 arm lengths.')

This ingenious nonsense was well received by

the members of the Florentine Academy, and Galileo got what he was looking for. The head of the Academy assured him that he would receive his backing when he applied for the professorship of mathematics at Bologna.

This post had fallen vacant after the death of Ignazio Danti, who had also held the post of Papal Cosmographer, which was practically the Church's only scientific appointment. This post was taken seriously, as it was difficult for the Church to deny the existence of America and China, even though they didn't appear in the Bible or the works of Aristotle. Danti even had the new Pontifical Meridian set in bricks into the stone floor of his office atop the Tower of Winds in the Vatican. Ships using this meridian to navigate in distant parts, and even observers in Europe, soon noticed that the seasons were becoming out of sync with the calendar. As a result, the Pope introduced the Gregorian calendar in 1582, advancing the date by ten days. (As this calendar was introduced over the years throughout Europe it provoked riots, with indignant mobs demanding back the ten days which had been robbed from their lives.) This bold introduction of the Gregorian calendar was a pointer to the way things might have been. Here the Church was ahead of current thinking – demonstrating that the coming conflict between the Church and science was unnecessary and could indeed have been avoided.

After the death of Danti, Galileo duly applied for the post of professor of mathematics at Bologna, but was turned down. This rejection hit him hard. It didn't dent his belief in his own abilities, but it gave him a much needed lesson in social reality. In order to succeed, you needed a powerful patron – no matter how good you were.

Galileo decided to ask his father to use his influence at court. If he could be granted a private audience with the Grand Duke Francesco I, then he would surely be able to persuade this fellow scientist to become his patron. But before Vincenzo could put out feelers, the scientific grand duke had agonizingly succumbed to science (or at least his vitriolic version of it). Francesco I was duly succeeded by his more reasonable brother, Ferdinand I. The court was ruthlessly purged of Francesco's coterie: trusted advisers were dismissed, procurers of rare medicaments were banished, and even disputatious musical theorists fell from favour.

Vincenzo was now too old to give lessons, and retired in grim disgrace.

Galileo realized he would have to look elsewhere for a patron. But where? His arrogant behaviour meant that he was hardly a popular figure on the social scene – and even on the scientific scene he only had a few admirers, who were of little social consequence. Galileo continued with his teaching, sometimes travelling as far afield as Siena to give a public lecture. In private, his mathematical studies were now reaching fruition. He had studied Archimedes' works *On the Equilibrium of Planes* and *On Conoids and Spheroids*. The former was the seminal work on mechanics, in which Archimedes set down the 'law of the lever'; in the latter he put this law into practice, determining the centre of gravity for various paraboloids (the solid formed when a parabola is rotated about its axis). Characteristically, Galileo set about bettering his hero, finding an original practical method for discovering the centres of gravity of various spheroids.

Galileo was not to publish this work for many years, but it did circulate in manuscript form amongst the mathematical fraternity throughout Italy, some of whom were so impressed that they referred to Galileo as 'the new Archimedes'. One of these was a local marquis called Guidobaldo del Monte, who just a year previously, in 1588, had published an extensive treatise on mechanics. Guidobaldo was no dilettante mathematician (his treatise was to become the standard work on mechanics in the following century), and he too was interested in the centre of gravity for various solids. Galileo travelled to see Guidobaldo, and they quickly became friends. Together they shared their findings on determining centres of gravity, and Guidobaldo was so impressed that he brought Galileo to the notice of the new Grand Duke of Tuscany, Ferdinando I.

The interest of aristocratic patrons is liable to fluctuate, but this was not to be the case with Guidobaldo. Galileo had at last found a constant and supportive patron. When the post of professor of mathematics at Pisa fell vacant, Guidobaldo immediately recommended Galileo, and he was accepted. Galileo was overjoyed – at last he had arrived. Only later did he discover that his salary was a mere 60 crowns (on a par with the earnings of a shopkeeper): hardly sufficient to support a man of Galileo's growing bulk, appetites and ambition.

The University of Pisa was unprepared for the return of its wayward son. The new professor of mathematics (who had previously failed to obtain a degree at this very university) arrived filled with new-found confidence. The 25-year-old don with flowing red hair and an argumentative manner quickly established himself as a popular figure. With the students, at any rate. The university authorities were mainly friars of unimpeachable orthodoxy and mediocrity. Galileo rejected both their sloth and their Aristotelian jargon. Likewise, he spurned their academic attire. Perennially scruffy, he refused to wear a gown – even going so far as to compose a student ditty about this:

'Only wear gowns
if you're a dim-wit who frowns,
it's the uniform for schools
who have to obey rules;
not allowed in the bordello
if you're that sort of fellow . . .'

The authorities were not amused.

It is during this period that Galileo may have conducted his legendary experiment from the top of the Leaning Tower of Pisa. This confirmed his previous insight regarding the hailstones. Objects of the same material but different weight were dropped from the tower, but all fell at the same speed – the heaviest ones didn't travel faster, as they should have done according to Aristotle.

This story is scientifically and characteristically apt, even if the evidence for it may be as nebulous as the theory it set out to disprove. If only for this reason, it is worth considering. Galileo wished to conduct a public demonstration of a flaw in Aristotle. This was important, for Aristotle's teachings were regarded as all-of-a-piece, scientifically speaking. Each element, each law, each assumption – all connected one with another. By demonstrating the falsity of one tenet, Galileo was hinting at the falsity of the whole – even if only inadvertantly.

As we shall see, Galileo himself was not suggesting anything so bold. What he was opposing was the Aristotelian outlook. Science dealt with the facts of the everyday world. These were associated with physical experience, rather than mental principles. Experiment came first: theory had to follow.

At this point it's worth noting that Galileo never actually discovered *why* the two bodies fall at the same rate. This was not explained until a century later, when Newton put forward his law of gravity.

This states that any body in the universe attracts another with a force which varies directly as a product of the masses and inversely as the square of the distance between them. Galileo's claim to fame here is that he relied upon experiment and results rather than theory.

The importance of what Galileo was doing was far more radical than he was willing to admit, even to himself – at least to begin with. Despite publicity stunts from the Leaning Tower, he continued to lecture on the physics of Aristotle. And this was no hypocrisy. To a large extent he appears to have believed in what he was saying. Take for instance his view of the universe. Copernicus had published his own theory, describing how the planets circled the sun, as far back as 1543. Galileo certainly knew about this, but remained convinced of the Aristotelian view as established by Ptolemy. This placed the earth firmly at the centre of the universe, with the sun, the moon and the planets orbiting about it.

At this period, Galileo believed in Archimedes *and* Aristotle. He could see that there were discrepancies between the essentially scientific view of Archimedes and the essentially philosophical view of Aristotle – but he felt sure that these would one day be reconciled.

During this period Galileo also wrote his first major work 'About Motion' (*De Motu*). In his lecture on Dante's Inferno to the Florentine Academy he had applied science to literature – now he was to reverse the process. But his motive was the same. The combination of these two subjects appealed to a wider audience. Galileo was ambitious; he wanted publicity.

De Motu tells the story of two friends, Alexander and Dominicus, who meet up one winter's morning on the banks of the Arno. They set out to walk along the river down to the sea, six miles away, to buy some fish for lunch. As they are walking they see a man in a boat, rowing upstream against the current, and this prompts them to a discussion about motion. Galileo's ideas are put into the mouth of Alexander, though in this early work they are expressed in uncharacteristically dry form, lacking the verve and wit of Galileo's actual personality.

Having dispensed with Aristotle's notion that bodies of different weight fall at different speeds, Galileo now proposed a different explanation, based on the findings of his Leaning Tower experiment.

Here Galileo demonstrated what was to become his other great scientific method – his ability to use other people's ideas. Galileo's explanation of how bodies of different weight fall at a similar speed had, in fact, been put forward almost 40 years previously by the Venetian physicist Battista Benedetti (who had himself 'adapted' it from Archimedes' principle of buoyancy). Galileo certainly knew the work of Benedetti, who was his most able Renaissance predecessor in the field of physics.

Like Galileo, Benedetti had a divided mind, which straddled Medieval and Renaissance ideas. He was both a first-rate scientist and an ace astrologer. Having predicted that he would die in 1592, he found himself on his deathbed in 1590 – but was able to discover a mistake in his earlier astrological computations which enabled him to die with his zodiacal faith intact. On occasion, Galileo too was to display a similar Italian flare with regard to discrepancies.

Galileo was to set out three laws of motion:

1. All bodies fall from the same height in equal times.

2. In falling the final velocities are proportional to the times.

3. The spaces fallen through are proportional to the squares of the times.

Galileo demonstrated these laws with his inclined plane experiments:

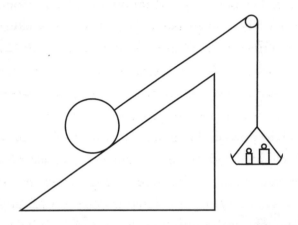

In Galileo's actual apparatus the ball moved down a groove in the inclined plane, thereby incurring the minimum of friction. The inclination of the plane didn't matter. Whatever its inclination (and thus, whatever the times taken) his laws applied.

According to Aristotle, a weight of 10 units would take ¹⁄₁₀ of the time taken by a weight of 1 unit. Galileo's experiments demonstrated this simply wasn't the case. But the Aristotelians remained unconvinced. Nature was derived from perfection (perfect ideas, abstraction), which meant that it *had* to obey Aristotle's perfect laws. Galileo's experiments were at best an anomaly (or, more ominously, mere trickery). Meanwhile, those who preferred reality pointed out that Galileo's experiments didn't *quite* match up with his laws. There were minor discrepancies. In fact, these were because Galileo didn't yet fully understand acceleration. He couldn't help noticing acceleration in his inclined plane experiments, but felt this wouldn't apply in free fall. He explained away what *appeared* to be acceleration here as due to a decreasing 'residual impressed force'. This was a notion which he 'derived' from the ancient Greek astronomer Hipparchus of Rhodes, who had lived in the second century BC and whose ideas were beginning to circulate in Renaissance Italy as part of the revival of classical learning. (An idea of the effect of this revival can be gauged from the fact that many of Hipparchus's scientific ideas, especially those on astronomy, remained in advance of those accepted in Italy at the end of the 16th century.)

There was of course another reason why falling bodies did not fall at *precisely* the same rate. This was due to air resistance. Galileo was aware of this, and suggested that direct equivalence would only take place in a vacuum. (This was to be given dramatic vindication in 1969, by the astronaut Neil Armstrong. On the surface of the Moon he dropped a hammer and a feather. Both fell to the ground at the same time, and Armstrong remarked: 'You see, Galileo was right.')

Using similar apparatus to that in the earlier diagram, Galileo also derived a law governing the equilibrium of weights on inclined planes (ie, when the situation is static in the apparatus and the weights balance one another). Here, Galileo's idea of static forces came uncannily close to anticipating Newton's third law of motion (which states that whenever a body exerts a force on another body, the second body exerts an equal and opposite force [or reaction] on the first body).

The recent introduction of gunpowder from China had stimulated interest in the study of projectiles. If gunnery was to develop from a largely hit-and-miss affair, it was necessary to predict the path of projectiles. According to Aristotle, a projectile's path resulted from two types of motion, the forced and the natural. The former was induced by the gunpowder, the latter 'naturally' pulled the projectile to earth.

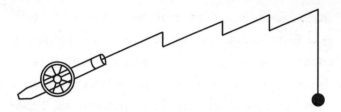

Galileo was able to show that according to his laws the projectile followed a parabolic course.

This was of course obvious to anyone who has ever thrown a stone – and watched its path up through the air and down through the greenhouse roof. So how on earth could the theorists have continued to maintain Aristotle's position for almost two millennia? This was largely due to the prevailing *attitude* towards the world, the entire structure of thought adopted by the medieval mind. According to this way of thinking, the world conformed to ideas. Practice conformed to theory. The truth was derived from the authority of these ideas. Aristotle's ideas were right, and therefore what happened *must* follow them. When this appeared not to be the case, it was either due to illusion or perversity (either in the observer or in the way of the world). It was the breaking of this mind-set – or *episteme*, in structuralist jargon – which was the beginning of the modern scientific age. Experience, experiment, facts, reality – these now became the truth. From now on theory had to follow. Galileo was to become a central figure in the growing (but largely unrecognized) revolution which was taking place.

Despite occasional borrowings, Galileo's *De Motu* was more original than any contemporary thinking on the subject of motion. Here, at last, was the work which could bring him widespread fame, riches, the admiration of his colleagues, the love of beautiful women and so forth – such as any scientist dreamt of. (This of course applies only to Renaissance scientists.) Yet Galileo never published this work. Why?

There were various reasons for this. (Though curiously, fear of accusations of plagiarism does not appear to have featured amongst them.) For a start, there were those niggling inconsistencies between his laws and his experimental findings. There had to be a way round these, he felt sure, but he hadn't yet found it. But the main reason Galileo didn't publish *De Motu* derives from something more central to his character. He was afraid. Like many larger-than-life personalities, Galileo was prey to inner uncertainties. Though he affected to dismiss his academic colleagues as hidebound mediocrities, he surreptitiously longed for their recognition. He was beset by the secret fear that his work would provoke ridicule, and that he would be regarded as a mere figure of fun. Galileo longed to be taken seriously – which didn't come easily to a man of his behaviour and habits. Disdaining to wear a gown, so that he wouldn't be refused entry to the bordellos, was hardly the kind of behaviour to endear him to his priestly academic colleagues. Such contradictions were never far below the surface in Galileo, and were to play an increasingly crucial role in both his reaction to the world and the world's reaction to him.

In 1591 Galileo's father died, leaving him to look after the family – six brothers and sisters, and an elderly complaining mother. His older sister, Virginia, had been promised a large dowry, and his brother, Michelangelo, had already become a feckless musician in constant need of 'sponsoring'. Meanwhile his mother insisted upon maintaining the family home in Florence, whose upkeep was a constant drain. Galileo already overspent his miserable salary, indulging his taste for experiments (in the culinary and amatory, as well as the scientific field). And to make matters worse, he now had few friends in Pisa. He had alienated his academic colleagues, but worse still, he had also exasperated the authorities by criticizing a plan for dredging the harbour at Livorno drawn up by Giovanni de Medici, the natural son of the Grand Duke. (Giovanni had drawn up a design for a large complex dredging machine, which Galileo dismissed as useless. Needless to say, his case was not helped when the machine was eventually built, and turned out to be just that. Galileo was never one for keeping his mouth shut.)

In 1592 the University of Pisa decided against renewing Galileo's three-year contract. Fortunately, at around this time the chair of mathematics at Padua fell vacant. Galileo applied for the job, once more strongly recommended by his aristocratic scientific patron, Guidobaldo del Monte. His application was also backed by the Grand Duke of Tuscany and the authorities of Pisa University, who evidently had their own reasons for wishing him to leave Tuscany. Galileo got the job.

The University of Padua was at this time one of the leading universities in Europe, attracting students from as far afield as Germany, Poland and England. (Shakespeare gleaned his background information on Italy from one of these students.) Padua fell within the domain of the Venetian Republic, which prudently chose not to interfere in university business. During this period Venice was a civilized easygoing spot, with little of the testosterone volatility which marred the political scene of other Renaissance republics. Not for nothing was it christened *La Serenissima*, 'the most serene'. (It was here that Casanova was to learn his trade, before his tiresomely monotonous behaviour caused him to be confined to a single bed, in a single dungeon.)

Venice was also the capital of a large maritime empire, which extended through the eastern Mediterranean, including the Ionian islands, Crete, and previously, Cyprus. This gave the city a cosmopolitan air, which Galileo found much to his liking. Padua was just 20 miles inland, and Galileo was soon spending his weekends sampling the delights of Venetian culture, both high and low.

But it wasn't all nights on the tiles. The circumstances of Galileo's family back in Florence meant that he was still strapped for cash. Indeed, during his holidays from Pisa over the years he had accumulated sizeable debts in Florence. So much so that his mother now wrote to warn him that one of his creditors 'is threatening to have you clapped in irons and cast into the debtors' dungeon as soon as you set foot in the city'. To supplement his university income Galileo once more engaged in private tutoring, and also put his practical skills to use, advising on various engineering projects and thinking up a number of inventions. He wrote instructions on how to improve battlements, designed an oil lamp for use in fortresses, and invented the first thermometer. The latter was an elementary affair involving a hand-warmed bulb inside which the air expanded, forcing water along a thin tube. As with many such inventions of genius, it was so simple as to appear obvious (afterwards). The modern thermometer merely incorporates a few refinements, such as high-expanding mercury and capillary tubing.

Galileo was ahead of his time. These inventions never quite turned into the money-spinners he confidently expected. Disheartened, he turned to

Guidobaldo del Monte for advice, and once again his patron-colleague came up trumps. Guidobaldo's brother was a general in the Venetian army, and was becoming increasingly vexed at the inaccuracy of his artillery. Was it possible for Galileo to design some lightweight instrument which could be used for calculating the trajectories of cannon-balls, and matching these to the distance and elevation of their targets?

Once again Galileo came up with a design of dazzling simplicity. His 'Geometric and Military Compass' was a masterpiece which could be adapted to a host of military and civilian uses. Basically, it consisted of two hinged bronze rulers engraved with lines, with a lower quadrant engraved with further lines.

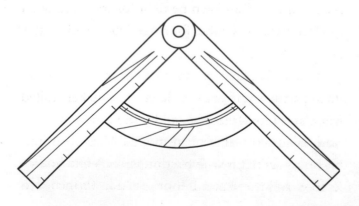

In order to calculate the trajectory of a projectile, one arm was placed inside the barrel of the gun. The artillery officer then aligned the rulers and read off the range. This could be done standing beside the barrel, rather than in front of it – a refinement that was to save the lives of many officers in this era of somewhat unpredictable artillery (and operators). Galileo's invention, now generally known as a sector, could also be adapted to a wide variety of civilian uses. In geometry, it could be used for mechanical tasks such as squaring circles, describing regular polygons, and dividing circumferences into equal parts. It could also be used for such problems as discovering the proportional weights of metals, transforming a given body of one metal into one of another with a similar weight, extracting cube roots (and it could even be used for transforming a paralleliped into a cube, for those who required this useful service).

At last Galileo was on to a winner. He went into partnership with a local toolmaker called Marc'antonio Mazzoleni, and started mass production. By 1600 Galileo had moved Mazzoleni into his house, with his wife becoming cook and housekeeper; and the ground floor was transformed into a factory for the manufacture of his military compasses. Galileo's invention was now being exported all over Italy, and he decided to write a handbook explaining its various uses. In all, Mazzoleni was to produce over 100 of these geometric and military compasses, which Galileo sold at 50 lire apiece (not including handbook). Production costs were as little as 15 lire. According to Galileo's accounts, Mazzoleni appears to have been paid less than half a crown a month, suggesting that this 'partnership' was somewhat unevenly balanced. But this all contributed to a good margin of profit – at least where the inventor-cum-chief-supervisor was concerned.

Then disaster struck. Galileo's general behaviour had already succeeded in making him enemies on the Padua campus, and his enthusiastic venture into the world of commerce put more noses out of joint. But where some disapproved, others were willing to go further. A conspiracy against Galileo was set up. When he eventually published the instruction handbook for his compass, he was immediately charged with plagiarism. Galileo couldn't believe his ears. Then, to his consternation, he discovered that a certain Baldassare Capra had already published a handbook on an identical geometric and military compass.

Galileo was beside himself. If Capra succeeded in this plagiarism case, his one successful business venture was over. He applied to the university authorities, who decided to take the matter very seriously (again, possibly for their own reasons, especially when it looked as if Galileo was in the wrong). After various investigations, it was discovered that Baldassare Capra was a 17-year-old youth who had been tutored by Galileo, and had used this opportunity to study the manuscript for Galileo's handbook. Capra was evidently just the fall guy. His book turned out to be a thinly disguised Latin version of Galileo's work (which was in Italian). The case collapsed, and Capra fled the republic for the safety of his home city, Milan. Galileo's fright was over, but he never forgot this incident. Even 25 years later – when he was famous throughout Europe, and Capra was ailing in the obscurity to which he aspired – Galileo was still expressing 'resentment and protest' in his work over this matter.

Around the same time as he invented his military compass, Galileo also invented a water pump operated by a horse. This could drain a large tract of land and distribute the water into over a dozen irrigation channels. Galileo had high hopes for his machine, confident that it would soon be put to use all over the Po Delta (where widespread rice production had been introduced a century or so earlier from China). With this in mind, Galileo took out a patent on his machine with the Venetian authorities – one of the earliest such commercial patents ever issued. But to no avail: this time no one was interested. The prototype of Galileo's ingenious water pump and mass irrigator ended up being sold on the cheap to a local aristocrat, who used it for watering his garden.

Despite such setbacks, life in Venice remained very much to Galileo's taste. He enjoyed the lively social scene, and it was here that he met a 25-year-old nobleman who was to become a lifelong friend. Gianfrancesco Sagredo may have been ten years younger than his new friend, but he was a man after Galileo's heart: an ebullient character of many parts, brilliant but curiously flawed. His family was distinguished – including a cardinal, the ambassador to Paris, the usual saint (*de rigeur* for all the best families), and an idiot who lived in a darkened room (another *sine qua non*). Sagredo himself occupied a pink Gothic palace with rose-tinted windows, by the Grand Canal near Rialto Bridge. Inside the palace, rare wolfhounds padded the sweeping marble staircases, parrots fluttered and squawked through the tapestried halls, and the finest courtesans in Venice were entertained in boudoirs outfitted solely for their purpose ('The Claudia Suite' etc). Occasionally, Sagredo would take up some minor public office – a foreign mission, a temporary governorship, head of a committee – but for the most part he preferred to follow his own intellectual pursuits.

Here was a man who loved wine, women and science. Galileo was entranced. Within months he and Sagredo were as close as brothers, and Galileo became a regular visitor to the weekend revels at Sagredo's palace.

Galileo's scientific treatises took on Sagredo's literary flourishes, and he learned to spice his scientific speculations with wit. Galileo had always aspired to literary grace, but the style had never quite matched the man. Now the slightly turgid delivery of *De Motu* became a thing of the past. His letters, his treatises, even his jottings, were never to be the same again.

Galileo's next important work was 'Mechanics' (*La Meccaniche*), which is in fact little more than a collection of his lecture notes to his students. In this he enlarges upon several of the ideas in *De Motu*, which he continued to develop throughout his life. Rather than follow the meanderings of this development, it's more useful here to understand what Galileo finally achieved in the field of mechanics.

Prior to Galileo, there had been little real conception of mechanics as such. What we now call mechanics had consisted merely of a number of unrelated theorems and facts. Once again, Archimedes had been the central figure here, with his *On the Equilibrium of Planes*, which set out the 'law of the lever' and established the centre of gravity of various conic sections. Other independent thinkers, mainly from the ancient Greek world, had contributed isolated snippets of mechanical learning. But nothing united this knowledge, establishing the field of mechanics as such, until Galileo came up with the notion of force. Here lay the key to it all. Unfortunately, Galileo never actually encapsulated this notion in a law, uniting the ideas of motion and force (though his work on dynamics gave undeniable evidence that he understood it). Indeed, his investigation of falling bodies, of equilibrium on inclined planes, and on the course of projectiles, points even further.

As we have already seen, Galileo's work on equilibrium hints that he knew Newton's third law of motion (concerning action and reaction being equal). His 'improvement' of Archimedes' notion of momentum, and his investigation of the courses of projectiles, suggests that he also probably knew Newton's first two laws of motion (that a body continues at rest or in uniform motion unless acted upon by an external force; and the rate of change of momentum of a moving body is proportional to the force acting upon it). By now it was apparent that Galileo had also taken on board the notion of acceleration. It was to be another lifetime before Newton formulated these findings in the form of laws, in the 1660s.

The secret of Galileo's success was yet another stroke of genius – so brilliantly simple that it now appears obvious to us. He combined mathematics and physics. Previously, these two subjects had been treated as largely independent. When they were combined – and the notion of force appeared – modern physics was born. This application of mathematical analysis to physics brought into being the idea of experiments, as we conceive of them today. That is, experimental science. Here, concrete practical experience could be abstracted into numerical and conceptual terms, results could be compared to see if they agreed with each other, and in consequence general laws could be formulated. Galileo called these practical tests *cimento*, which in Italian means 'ordeal'. (Our word experiment similarly derives from an old French word, meaning 'to put to trial'.)

As with many of Galileo's practical achievements, others have claimed priority here. And with every justification. Such ideas were 'in the air'. The long-established medieval *episteme* was crumbling. Modern science was being born all over Europe in individual cells and dens. (To grace such habitats with the name laboratory gives the wrong impression. Scientists are seldom ahead of their time where interior decor is concerned, and the Renaissance was to be no exception. Their places of work still appeared to be inspired by the medieval dungeon rather than the Palladian villa.) To call such scientific thinkers ahead of their time is ungenerous. They were, in fact, doing nothing less than creating an entirely new time. A new mind-set was gelling. Indicative of this is the fact that many 'simultaneous' discoveries were arrived at without any resort to plagiarism. Here indeed was a new development. One relevant example will suffice. Galileo completed his geometric and military compass in 1597. A year later, the 38-year-old Elizabethan mathematician, Thomas Hood, produced his uncannily similar sector in London months before his tragic death. In the same year, the Dutch mathematician Dirk Borcouts, who corresponded with Descartes, manufactured in Utrecht a bronze sector which can still be seen in a local museum today.

Galileo was merely the major figure, combining conceptions which were superior in quality as well as quantity. Viz: the application of mathematical analysis, experiment, conceptual penetration (eg, the notion of force), immense technical skill, and strokes of genius which eluded lesser practitioners. He may not always have been the first (even when he liked to think so), but as we shall see he was invariably the finest. Galileo was now on the threshold of his most spectacular discovery of all.

But first he was to make a more down to earth

discovery. Some time during 1599, at one of the revels in Sagredo's palace, Galileo met Marina Gamba. In the eloquent Italian of the day, Marina was *una donna di facile costume* (which may be translated equally poetically as a woman whose clothes came off easily). She was also of striking appearance and possessed of a fiery temperament. Little else is known about her, except that she came from the back streets of San Sofia (behind Sagredo's palace), was almost certainly illiterate, and was 21 years old. Galileo was used to women of easy virtue, but was not inclined to emotional attachment. The effervescent but knowing Marina evidently understood just how to handle the 35-year-old Galileo, and in no time he'd fallen for her. She became Galileo's mistress, and he set her up in a house by the market around the corner from his Padua home. Marina had found her meal ticket, and Galileo had succeeded in losing his emotional virginity.

In accordance with the mores of the time, there was no question of marriage between the university professor and the backstreet beauty. This would have provoked more social outrage than either of them was prepared to endure. Theirs was a commonplace arrangement in an era when class delineation was considered a matter of great importance.

Within a year Marina produced a daughter, who was registered in the customary frank style by the Church: 'Virginia, daughter of Marina of Venice, born of fornication, 13th August 1600.' Galileo and Marina were to have three children in all. She never took up permanent residence in the same house as Galileo, though his servants became godparents to their children. And despite the absence of his name on the birth register, Galileo loved and cherished all three of his children. Indeed, he seems to have been a particularly good father, inspiring equal affection in return.

The only one who disapproved of this arrangement was Mama. Just because he sent money to support her in Florence, didn't mean her approval could be bought. When Mama visited Galileo in Padua, and found Marina hanging around in the kitchen, she intuited her status at once. Galileo's previous inability to commit himself emotionally almost certainly stemmed from the commitment demanded by his difficult mother. But now it was evident that Mama had been usurped in his emotions. Her precious 35-year-old boy had been stolen from her by some nasty illiterate little tart. Right from the start of Mama's visit to Padua, the sparks began to fly. Marina was a tough customer, but Mama was not the sort to be cowed. The clichéd Freudian-Italian drama ensued. The arguments soon became slanging matches. These then descended into shrieking brawls and hair-tugging. Galileo was forced to separate the two women in his life, and despatch them to their respective homes. But not before Mama had bribed one of his servants to spy on his activities with Marina. From now on Mama was sent regular reports containing evidence of his heinous ingratitude and infidelity to the only woman deserving of his affection. (Not for nothing did Greek tragedies, such as *Oedipus Rex*, undergo a resurgence of popularity in Renaissance Italy.)

But there were other views on what occupied the centre of the universe. For some years Galileo had experienced doubts about the Ptolemaic view of cosmology, which placed the Earth at the centre of the universe and accorded with Aristotelian ideas. Quite early during his stay in Padua, he seems to have inclined to the Copernican view that the Earth and the planets circled the Sun.

The revolution brought about by Copernicus was to be central to the emerging scientific age. The Polish astronomer Copernicus had died in 1543, after spending most of his working life as a cathedral canon at the small town of Frauenburg (now Frombork) on the Baltic coast of Poland. This virtual sinecure had provided him with the financial security and leisure to pursue his obsession with astronomy. Curiously, neither his observations nor his mathematics had much depth. (On average he carried out observations less than once a year, and his calculations of the planetary orbits were simply wrong.) The idea of a heliocentric system appealed to Copernicus largely because of its elegance.

In other words, this idea which spelt the end of the medieval era was in fact a characteristically medieval conception. It trusted in the realm of ideas, rather than experience (where ironically common sense observed the Sun rising and setting, rather than being stationary). Likewise, Copernicus defeated the early objections to his system by advancing ideas rather than observational evidence. Indeed, the hard facts remained on the side of his detractors — who pointed out that if the Earth moved around the Sun, the stars should exhibit parallax. In other words, their positions in the sky should change. But they didn't. Sitting it out in his chilly cathedral on the edge of the frozen Baltic, Copernicus found many long hours in which to ponder these arguments, and come up with ingenious counter-arguments. In this instance he argued, on no *evidence* whatsoever, that the reason the stars didn't move was because they were so far away. Much, much further away than anyone had previously thought. Copernicus was the first modern thinker to introduce the notion that the universe occupied a space bordering on the infinite (though this had in fact been suggested all but 2,000 years previously by a number of ancient Greek astronomers). So this universe-transforming modern idea originated not from evidence, or indeed from reason, but from sheer sophistry. It sprung from that most medieval of skills: the ability to argue your way out of a tight corner, no matter how overwhelming the evidence against you.

This approach – the Indian Rope Trick method – has undergone something of a revival in modern learning. (Viz: the continuing arguments for Steady State, a Theory of Everything, the End of History etc.) But it has yet to introduce an idea of Copernican status, capable of changing our entire mind-set, though the overwhelming evidence from the past suggests that this is precisely where the next such idea will come from. It is on such apparently unplausible ideas that all limited world-views (which includes our own) have chosen to float. (The curved space of relativity is no less incredible than a motionless Sun.)

But back to the Renaissance, and the previous giant leap forward for the human mind. Where Copernicus was concerned, the Aristotelians had one final ace up their monastic sleeves. When the Earth was the centre of the universe, things automatically fell towards it by 'natural' force. If the Earth wasn't the centre of the universe, what was it that impelled everything from wine glasses to guano to fall to earth? Copernicus had no answer to this. (The answer, when it came, was of course Newton's gravity − the first real step towards a Theory of Everything. But it was Copernicus who opened up the *possibility* of such a thing.)

Copernicus circulated his ideas amongst fellow scholars, but was against publishing them, despite the urging of friends. He enjoyed being a cathedral canon, and wished to go on doing so. Only when he knew he was dying did he eventually relent. On the day of his death, May 24th 1543, he was finally presented with the first printed copy of his epoch-making book 'About the revolutions of the heavenly bodies', (*De Revolutionibus Orbium Coelestium*).

In keeping with his underlying Aristotelian approach, Copernicus maintained that the orbits of the planets had to be precisely circular and take place at unvarying speeds. Such idealistic notions soon became increasingly difficult to square with actual astronomical observation, which was becoming something of a scientific craze. (Indicatively, the first scientific revolution amongst the ancient Greeks was accompanied by a similar craze for astronomy.)

By far the most important observer of the pre-telescope era was the Dane Tycho Brahe, who observed a new star in the constellation of Cassiopeia in 1572. This was in fact a nova (an exploding star), the first of its kind that had been visible since 134 BC. For a year this star was brighter than the planet Venus, yet it was undeniably a 'fixed' star of the firmament ie, not one of the mobile bodies which made up the solar system.

The arrival of this star on the scene caused further consternation amongst the orthodox non-thinkers. According to Aristotle the heavens were perfect and unchangeable, being composed of 'quintessence' (the 'fifth essence' which was latent in all things). There could be no such thing as a new star, any more than an old one could disappear. Objects such as comets, which seemed to contradict such a view, were cunningly explained away. These phenomena did not belong to the heavens at all. They took place in the sub-lunar region closest to earth – and were thus meteorological events and not stars.

Never ones to shirk a good argument, the Aristotelians soon had an answer for Tycho Brahe's new star. It was in fact merely a 'tail-less comet', and thus it too was simply a meteorological phenomenon. But the trouble was it didn't move (which was the main distinguishing feature of a comet). It was undoubtedly a star, and equally undoubtedly it had suddenly appeared out of nowhere. (It is now named 'Tycho's Star' after him.) For the time being a compromise was agreed: this so-called star, which was undeniably there, would have to be regarded as an oddity.

Tycho Brahe was something of an oddity himself. Whilst still a baby, he was kidnapped by a childless uncle and brought up in a remote Danish castle. At the age of 12 he witnessed a solar eclipse, and at once swore to devote his life to science. From then on he took science very seriously indeed, so much so that when he was 19 he fought a duel over a mathematical argument, and lost his nose in the process. Further scientific dedication produced the silver nose which he designed for himself. (This provided the model for Lee Marvin's similar appendage in the western *Cat Ballou*.) Brahe spent over 20 years in his underground telescope-less observatory on the tiny island of Hven, off the Danish coast. During this period he mapped the position of 777 stars.

Towards the end of his life the eccentric Brahe was enticed to Prague, where the mad Holy Roman Emperor Rudolph II became his patron. Here Brahe set up an observatory in a Bohemian castle and continued his research, aided by a difficult young assistant called Johannes Kepler, who suffered from mange, worms, and the occasional delusion that he was a dog. When Brahe died in 1601, Kepler inherited his vast store of documents mapping the stars. As is the wont of assistants, Kepler was soon making improvements on his master's work. He noticed a discrepancy in Brahe's observations of Mars, which he had tried to fit to its circular orbit, as proposed by Copernicus. Eventually he worked out that Mars, and all the other planets, in fact orbited the Sun in ellipses. The Sun was at one of the two foci of the ellipse, and the planet speeded up as it came closer to the Sun. Drawing on calculations he had included in one of his previous treatises *The New Solid Geometry of Wine Barrels*, he worked out his famous law: 'A line connecting a planet and the sun will sweep out equal areas in equal times as the planet moves on its orbit.'

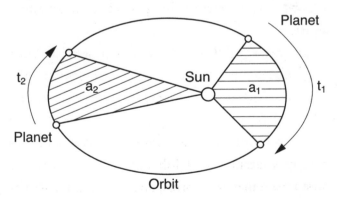

When $t_1 = t_2$, $a_1 = a_2$.

Galileo began corresponding with Kepler

around the turn of the 17th century. He confessed to Kepler that he believed Copernicus's helio-centric picture to be correct, but refrained from admitting this in public because he was afraid of becoming a laughing stock amongst his academic colleagues at Padua, who still remained almost exclusively Aristotelians. Galileo *believed* that the Copernican view was correct, but didn't realize that by this stage Kepler was already on his way both to *confirming* it and *improving* upon it.

In 1604 another supernova appeared in the sky. Within days Galileo heard of this, and was out observing the new phenomenon. Just like Tycho's Star, this too soon became so bright that it was even visible during the day. Galileo wrote to astronomical observers throughout Europe about this star. They wrote back confirming its position, and the fact that it exhibited no parallax. Their observations and measurements showed that the new star was not part of the solar system, it was in the distant heavens.

Galileo began a series of public lectures on the star, pointing out how it disproved Aristotelian notions about the heavens. As a result he became embroiled in a public feud with the professor of philosophy at Padua, Cesare Cremonini, a leading

Aristotelian who had previously been a close friend of Galileo. For a paltry mathematician to cast aspersions on Aristotle – upon whom all thought, learning and philosophy was based – was more than Cremonini could tolerate. And besides, Galileo's arguments were simply faulty. Cremonini pointed out that physical laws and measurements only applied to the sub-lunar sphere, on Earth. The heavens above, which included all the planets and the stars, were just not subject to the same physical laws. Earth-bound measurements of this heavenly sphere only *appeared* to contradict Aristotle – they were in fact inapplicable, and thus irrelevant. For the time being, it was impossible for Galileo to deny such arguments. He had no convincing proof to the contrary. (Galileo did not know of Kepler's work on the elliptical orbits of the planets. This showed that mathematics applied to the heavens just as it did on earth, suggesting that the same physical laws held true in both realms.)

Galileo was now 40, yet to his chagrin lasting fame and fortune still eluded him. Others of paltry stature continued to make a name for themselves, or earn more than him. His salary at Padua was just 500 crowns: half that of the professor of philosophy.

Despite his series of brilliant inventions – agricultural devices, military knick-knacks, medical instruments – none of them had quite struck gold. (Others had by this stage moved into the military compass business, after it had been discovered that Galileo's patent didn't apply to the rival versions of this instrument which had been produced before he 'invented' it.) Galileo now had to provide for a family of three growing children, a wilful mistress, and recalcitrant Mama at home in Florence. To say nothing of his own disordered habits.

Galileo was constantly importuning his friends for cash. He even pestered Sagredo to pressure the Venetian authorities on his behalf, for a raise in salary. Even those who most enjoyed his company were beginning to find him a bit of a bore sometimes. Galileo was convinced of his outstanding superiority as a scientist, as an inventor, and as a personality. Yet the world obstinately refused to recognize his brilliance. The more timid inner man increasingly craved reassurance. It was time for his mid-life crisis. Filled with emotion and self-pity, Galileo petitioned the Grand Duke of Tuscany, Ferdinand I, for a post. Perhaps they would appreciate him more at home in Florence. Ferdinand I still regarded Galileo as one of Tuscany's finest ornaments: 'the greatest mathematician in Christendom.' Yet so far he had not been persuaded to give more concrete evidence of his esteem. But this time Galileo's luck was in. The Grand Duke needed a tutor for his son and heir, the 15-year-old Cosimo. Galileo was allowed the free run of the Villa Fratolino, and spent a pleasant sabbatical living a life of luxury, at the same time endearing himself to his young charge. But after this it was back to Padua and his creditors.

Four years later Galileo was to repay this generosity in unwonted fashion. Ferdinand's wife, the Grand Duchess Cristina, was under the impression that her husband regarded Galileo as a great astrologer, rather than a great astronomer. So when her husband fell ill, she begged Galileo to cast his horoscope. Not wishing to fall from favour, Galileo duly produced the usual star-studded formula. According to the constellations all was well: the movements of the heavens decreed that Ferdinand would soon recover, and was destined to live for many years to come . . . Alas, Ferdinand was dead within the month. It looked as if another avenue of opportunity was closed.

When Galileo arrived in the city of Venice in July 1609 for a summer weekend break, he heard the rumour that was passing around town. A Dutch spectacle maker in Middelburg had invented an instrument that could make distant objects appear close up. This consisted of two lenses aligned in a tube, and could make a church steeple many miles away appear as if it was just across a field. One of these marvels, known as a perspicillium, had already been demonstrated in Milan.

Galileo at once grasped the basic principle behind this invention, and equally quickly realized its commercial potential. When he discovered that the perspicillium had no patent, he returned forthwith to Padua to attack the problem. 'The first night after my return, I solved it,' he later boasted, 'and on the following day I constructed the instrument.' A typical exaggeration – but there's no doubt that he worked fast. Within a fortnight Galileo had built an instrument capable of threefold magnification, and quickly improved this to the power of ten. He then set out for Venice, to demonstrate his instrument before the Doge and his ruling council. Galileo explained how vital such a device could be for the defence of a maritime city such as Venice. Enemy ships could be spotted hours before any attack.

The Doge and his counsellors were hugely impressed. It quickly became apparent that they would be willing to pay almost anything to lay their hands on such an instrument. But during his long years in the Venetian Republic Galileo had at last learned a thing or two about politics – not least from important friends such as Sagredo, who knew how the Venetian political system worked from the inside. Galileo presented his perspicillium to the Doge as a gift, for the defence of Venice. Galileo's reward was not long in coming. Within a month the Doge had ordered Galileo's university salary to be doubled to 1000 crowns, with an immediate gift of 500 crowns. Also, his professorship at Padua was extended for the rest of his life.

Fortunately these arrangements were quickly finalized, and proved irrevocable. Only a week or so later cheap perspicillia began flooding the market, and were soon on sale in Venice for a few scudi. Galileo dismissed these as mere toys. Their magnification was only a few times, whereas that of his instruments was much, much more. Galileo had in fact by now produced a perspicillium with magnification of 32 times.

Galileo decided it was time to rename this new instrument, and claim it as his own. Word quickly spread of Galileo's wondrous new invention, which he called a 'telescope'. This comes from the Greek words for 'at a distance' and 'to see'. Much like his invention, this name too was not in fact Galileo's. The name telescope was first used by the multi-talented Prince Cesi, who not only founded the first modern scientific academy, the *Accademia dei Lincei* in Rome, but also proposed a rational system for the classification of plants well over a century before Linnaeus, the founder of modern botany. Galileo's justification for his claim to have invented the telescope, when presented with incontrovertible evidence to the contrary, was typically robust: 'Any idiot can discover such a thing by accident. I was the one who discovered it by reason, which requires genuine originality.' Not for nothing had he cut his teeth arguing with Aristotelians.

There is no doubt that Galileo transformed the original crude invention into a powerful observational tool. Amongst other refinements he introduced was a method for checking the lense curvature which enabled the telescope to be used for efficient astronomical observation. Galileo had quickly understood the possibilities of using the telescope in this fashion, though again he was not in fact the first to do so.

By the time Galileo raised his telescope to the heavens, the English scientist Thomas Harriot was already mapping the Moon. Harriot was a remarkable man, in many fields. He undertook a comprehensive investigation of the 'naturall inhabitants' of Virginia, was a member of the 'School of Night' along with Sir Walter Raleigh and the playwright Christopher Marlowe, and was involved in the Gunpowder Plot. His intellectual life was even more fascinating: after mapping the Moon he went on to establish himself as one of the leading astronomical observers of the age. He also produced a simplified notation which transformed algebra, and he became an enthusiast for 'drinking' tobacco smoke as a panacea. Harriot was typical of the geniuses being thrown up by the seismic shift taking place in the European mind.

As we have seen, an entirely new age was emerging. This is bewildering enough for us in the

20th century, where the process has been almost continuous. In an era when such a thing had not happened for many centuries, this was to be profoundly divisive. Some looked to the future, others were determined to retain the old certainties. As both Harriot and the invention of the telescope show, Galileo was far from being alone – though he often felt so. The sheer quality of Galileo emerges when we understand that he shone amidst such a highly competitive context. It was the depth of his perception and his originality (in developing if not always creating), which gave him the edge in both practical and theoretical work. Though not as great as Newton, he was to be his worthy predecessor.

Up until this point it could be argued that Galileo had not fully realized his potential. Only in his 40s did he emerge as a transcendent European figure – on a par with the likes of the philosopher-mathematician Descartes, Harvey (who discovered the circulation of the blood), and Kepler. These were the men who bridged what might be called the Age of Leonardo and that of Newton. Galileo's emergence was to bring him many of the ephemeral rewards which he had so long craved, but it was also to test his character in a way he had not foreseen.

Galileo now began exploring the heavens with his telescope. He saw himself as the new Columbus, no less. And the discoveries he was to make were almost equally sensational. Before this period, knowledge of the actual planets and the stars had remained almost at a standstill for around three-and-a-half millenia. The Babylonians gazing into the star-filled night sky from atop their ziggurats had taken astronomical observation with the naked eye to its limits.

The night Galileo put his telescope to his eye he saw a Moon transformed. Instead of a radiant semi-circular disc he saw a large and mysterious spherical body, bisected by a shadow whose precise edge was rendered ragged by the rough surface of the planet. Close examination of its surface revealed unmistakable round craters, mountain ranges, and what looked like seas. (This was the end of Aristotelian astronomy, he realized. The heavenly bodies were not perfect spheres at all.) When Galileo turned his telescope to the Milky Way, it was transformed from a diaphanous haze to a vast rash of stars.

Galileo was soon undertaking a systematic exploration of the solar system. Here he made further sensational discoveries. Jupiter had satellites! These new moons he christened *Sidera Medicea* (the Medici Stars) in honour of his enamoured pupil (who had now become Grand Duke). He also observed the 'phases of Venus' – similar to the phases of the Moon, as it waxes and wanes. This gave incontrovertible evidence that Venus circled the Sun (and also confirmed that the Earth did likewise). Galileo observed the Sun, and found that it had black spots 'which appeared to consume themselves'. These not only dissolved, but appeared seemingly at random, taking on all kinds of shapes 'like clouds'.

He made drawings of Saturn, then thought to be the furthest planet in the solar system.

He recorded: 'Saturn is not a single star, but three together . . . almost touching, with a small dark space between them.' He concluded: 'The furthest planet is a triple sun.' What was so astonishing was not that Galileo had mistaken Saturn's rings, but that he had been able to observe the planet in such detail in the first place, given his severely limited apparatus. Anyone who has attempted to observe Saturn through a 32 magnification telescope of the period will understand the full quality of Galileo's findings – which must have required long eye-bulging hours of observation, perceptive scientific imagination and inspired guesswork in almost equal proportions. Given his limited understanding of the universe, his findings were little short of miraculous.

In 1610 Galileo published all this new information in 'The Starry Messenger' (*Siderius Nuncius*). This short, stylish work was written in Latin, and became an overnight sensation amongst the Latin-reading classes (ie, all who had received an education, which was invariably conducted in this unpopular language). As with all Galileo's works, there were the inevitable objectors. The Jesuit astronomer Christoph Scheiner had built his own telescope in Bavaria, with which he too had seen spots on the Sun (some time before Galileo observed them). Father Schiener's superior had not been impressed, however, declaring: 'I have read

all the works of Aristotle and found nothing re-
sembling what you describe . . . Your spots on the
Sun are defects of your optical instruments or your
eyes.' Scheiner had thought differently: from his
superior, and from Galileo. In his view, what he
had seen were tiny planets circling close to the Sun
– but he was forced to publish this information
anonymously.

Galileo reacted vigorously to Scheiner's legiti-
mate suggestion that it was he who had discovered
sunspots. Once again the Aristotelians, the Jesuits,
the Papal authorities, his enemies, his creditors –
everyone was ganging up on him. Filled with
bombastic pride at becoming the famous author of
'The Starry Messenger', the sensation of Europe,
he remained riven by the inner uncertainties that
generated his paranoia. As the man increased in
stature, so did his paranoia. His replies to Scheiner
(and several others who offered modest objections)
were insufferable. Galileo was making himself further unnecessary enemies.

But at least his situation in Padua was now secure
– for life. So it came as something of a surprise to
the Venetian authorities and the generous Doge
when they heard that Galileo had decided to quit

the Most Serene Republic. In 1610 Cosimo de Medici had duly succeeded as Grand Duke – whereupon he had offered his former tutor the job of 'first philosopher and mathematician' in Tuscany. Along with the job went palatial accomodation at the Villa Bellosguardo on a hill overlooking Florence. Galileo decided this was an offer he would not refuse. Understandably: it meant no more tutoring, or delivering lectures on Aristotelian twaddle and Ptolemaic cosmological nonsense. No more political intriguing or the need to butter up powerful mediocrities. In his villa in the hills, sheltered by the patronage of the Grand Duke, he would be above mere politics. He could now devote all his time to research.

Galileo packed up and left Padua, taking his two daughters and young son with him, but leaving behind their mother. The end of Venice meant the end of Marina. This apparent heartlessness appears to have been a mutually agreed arrangement, or at least a socially accepted custom. Within a year Marina was happily married – suggesting the absence of heartbreak and the presence of a dowry (indications of both sides of the coin of Galilean behaviour). The one he would miss most of all was, of course, Sagredo. Opportunities for men behaving badly were not so available in Tuscany, whose *louche* era of decline still lay on the future horizon. Galileo and Sagredo would remain in correspondence, exchanging letters monthly, sometimes even weekly, until Sagredo died ten years later.

Galileo's researches proceeded apace, his intellect now free for equally progressive theorizing. He was soon able to predict the eclipses of Jupiter's moons, whose movement indicated the annual movement of the Earth around the Sun. (This was to be Galileo's strongest observational evidence to back the Copernican system.) He now drew up accurate tables outlining the future positions of Jupiter's moons and their frequent eclipses. These he suggested could be used by ships at sea to overcome the problem of establishing their longitude. (In the event Galileo's method proved impractical, and this problem was not solved until the revolution in chronometry over a century later.)

Curiously, despite his accurate observation of the solar system, Galileo rejected Kepler's evidence of elliptical planetary orbits. Throughout his life Galileo continued to hold to the Aristotelian notion that planetary orbits were circular. Yet this didn't stop him from coming up with original ideas on the mechanics of orbiting planets. He suspected the inertial path of a planet around the Sun was due to some kind of magnetism. His papers reveal that he was on the verge of conceiving of gravity as a universal force. However, he dismissed this notion – strangely, for the same reason as Descartes. They both regarded it as an 'occult' force (ie, a meta-physical rather than a scientific explanation). Galileo may have been hampered by vestigial ideas of 'inertia' and Aristotle's 'natural' force (attracting everything to the central Earth), but his application of physics to the motion of the planets was an epochal step. Kepler had applied mathematics to the universe, now Galileo showed that the Earth's laws of physics were also universal.

'Earthly laws apply in the heavens.' This was an adage too far – ears began pricking up in the offices of the Vatican. But Galileo remained unconcerned. By 1611 he had become such a celebrated figure that he was invited to Rome to demonstrate his new telescope at the Papal Court. The pontifical worthies were so impressed that Galileo decided it was time for him to 'come out' as a Copernican. He published a short work on sunspots, couched in stylish Italian, showing how these proved that the Ptolemaic system was wrong. This soon became a bestseller, especially amongst students in the universities. The Aristotelian academics quickly recognized the threat. If things went on like this, they'd soon all be out of a job. The academics and clerics began mustering their considerable polemical skills. Meanwhile others started putting out more covert political feelers. Something had to be done about this man Galileo.

The Aristotelians quite correctly pointed out that the Copernican heliocentric system conflicted with views of the universe put forward in the Bible. The Church realized it would have to act. Such heresy could not be tolerated.

This entire conflict between the Church and science was historically inevitable (even if it was, in another sense, completely unnecessary). During the Dark Ages, Christianity alone had kept Western civilization alive. Knowledge and culture had been preserved in isolated Christian communities – whilst in the outside world the Vandals, the Visigoths, the Vikings and the like went about doing what they were best at (eg, vandalism, rape and pillage, discovering America etc). As knowledge spread during the early Middle Ages, it spread from one source: the Church. By the time of the intellectual stasis of the High Medieval era the Church had, almost unwittingly, annexed all knowledge. Come the intellectual revival of the Renaissance, the Church found itself saddled with more than it had bargained for. Unwilling to relinquish this powerful monopoly, it decreed that science had to agree with its teachings. Progressive thought was harnessed to static intellectual practice. Something had to give. It was Galileo's misfortune that he was to become an emblematic figure in this struggle.

By a curious reversal, late 20th century science now finds itself in a remarkably similar position to religion in the early 17th century. Science considers itself master of *all* knowledge. Any knowledge that does not obey the rules of science is dismissed – as metaphysics, mysticism, mere psychology, economics or some such. All knowledge *has* to be scientific, and scientists now even take it upon themselves to pronounce on God – what he is, whether he exists, whether there is even 'room' for him etc. Will religion ever recover from this humiliation – or will some catastrophic rethink cause science similarly to rue its hubris? Science may well have overstepped the mark in its attempt to incorporate the spiritual and philosophical concerns of humanity, though whether it will suffer the same eclipse as religion remains to be seen. Such mega-historical considerations are worth bearing in mind as we (along with Galileo) enter the fray in one of history's great intellectual dogfights. The past was once the present, just as much as the present will one day be the hopelessly prejudiced and laughable past.

Meanwhile back in the 17th century . . . The anti-Galilean forces got off to a great start. Aristotelian clerics were soon delivering hell-raising sermons all over Italy, railing against the 'mathematicians'. Alas, what they were really denouncing was mathematics itself – which was undeniable. But in the wider sense this was of course a power struggle. The Church was struggling to maintain its dwindling pan-European influence, to say nothing of its pan-European income. This latter remained higher than most national budgets – deriving vast sums from such wheezes as the sale of indulgences (which absolved sins and promised the bearer free entry to heaven).

Where the likes of Galileo were concerned, the Church still had some heavy guns. Galileo was secretly denounced to the Inquisition for making blasphemous pronouncements. His belief in atomism posed a significant threat to the central doctrine of the Eucharist. If wine and wafers consisted of atoms, they could not become the blood and body of Christ. Galileo did his best to argue his way out of this tight corner. Writing to the authorities in Rome, he pointed out that already the Church had tacitly agreed to interpret the scriptures allegorically when they contradicted scientific reality. He asked them to have regard for 'the agonizing quandry in the soul of people who find themselves utterly convinced by a mathematical or scientific proof, only to discover that it is a sin to believe in such a thing'. In no time Galileo found himself being sucked deeper and deeper into the quagmire of Vatican politics. (Although the appellation byzantine originally derived from the notorious machinations and complex inner workings of the Eastern Church, its Western counterpart was no slouch in such matters.)

Eventually Galileo decided it would be politic to visit Rome to plead his case. But the chief theologian of the Church, Cardinal Robert Bellarmine, remained unconvinced by the rational arguments of the greatest scientist of his age. In the cardinal's view, mathematics had nothing to do with reality – and had no place in dealings with this sphere. This ancient Greek belief derived from the time of Plato, and had already been exploded a couple of centuries later by Archimedes. (Though owners of fruit stalls may have felt they had a prior claim here.) Unfortunately, between Plato and Archimedes had come Aristotle. He had accepted the Platonic view, and that meant it was accepted by the Church – *and would go on being so.*

The Church was having enough trouble fighting off Protestants, without having scientists to worry about. In 1616 Cardinal Bellarmine determined to resolve this matter once and for all. Copernicus's great work, 'About the Revolutions of the Heavenly Bodies', (*De Revolutionibus Orbium Coelestium*), was placed on the Index of banned books, and the Cardinal drew up a decree pronouncing that the Copernican system was both 'false and erroneous'. (One was evidently not enough.) Galileo was summoned to a private audience shortly before the edict was made public.

Here he was solemly warned that he must not 'hold or defend' Copernicanism, though he could still discuss it as a 'mathematical supposition'. (Presumably to do one would have been false, but to do the other would have been merely erroneous.)

Galileo licked his wounds and returned to the seclusion of his villa in Tuscany. The logical conundrum of the Church's position was best left alone, he decided. Though he still privately maintained: 'The Bible shows the way to go to heaven, not the way the heavens go.'

For the next seven years Galileo continued his scientific work in private, only publishing the occasional uncontroversial scientific treatise – on such things as tides, and comets. Yet his explanations of these phenomena remained *implicitly* controversial. The way Galileo accounted for the tides – in fact, wrongly – required the movement of the world, both on its axis and around the Sun. Likewise, he insisted that comets were not sublunar, which thus destroyed the notion of the unchanging Aristotelian heavens.

But Galileo was temperamentally unsuited to the quiet life. When the Jesuit Father, Orazio Grassi, published a highly influential pamphlet on comets which pooh-poohed Galileo's theories in favour of the Ptolemaic system, Galileo could contain himself no longer.

In 1632, at the age of 59, he published his reply in the form of a treatise entitled *Saggiatore* (usually known in English as the 'Assayer'). This work is much more than the rubbishing of some ingenious scientific ignoramus. In it Galileo puts forward his philosophical views on matter. He distinguishes between its primary qualities, such as those that can be measured scientifically, and its secondary qualities which can only be perceived, such as taste and smell. This distinction predates the work of the English philosopher John Locke by well over half a century. Locke was the founder of empiricism, which brought philosophy in line with the scientific achievements of Newton. Not only did Galileo lay the foundations for Newton's conception of gravity, but he also understood the import of what he was doing. He foresaw the philosophical implications of his scientific advances a generation before the philosophers. (Imagine a 19th century scientist coming up with an embryo conception of relativity, and also laying the foundations for Wittgenstein's philosophy.) In the

'Assayer' Galileo also expressed a view which, curiously, did in fact impress and influence Einstein. He declared that the 'Book of Nature is . . . written in mathematical characters', which was to become an article of faith in Einstein's description of the universe – relying as it did on speculation in mathematical terms, rather than experiment.

However, just to be on the safe side Galileo decided to dedicate his book to the glory of the new pope, Urban VIII. This was more than just tactful sycophancy. Urban VIII, in his previous guise as Cardinal Maffeo Barberini, had been introduced to Galileo by the Grand Duke of Tuscany at his court as early as 1611. Although Barberini was a devout Aristotelian, he had been so impressed by Galileo's views that he had written a gushing poem about him:

'We look up into the sky,
and what is it that we spy?
Father Saturn with his ears,
the Milky Way with all its tears.
And each discovered by your glass,
O learned Galileo! . . .' etc

Barberini had an expansive intellect, which was capable of embracing both astronomy and astrology – as well as the seemingly incompatible Copernican and Ptolemaic systems. This feat evidently impressed Galileo, leading him to believe that he was on to a winner where the new pope was concerned.

In 1624 Galileo set off once more for Rome, confident that the new pope would soon absolve him from his niggling promise to Cardinal Bellarmine to keep mum about Copernicus. But Urban VIII was more than just a skilled intellectual contortionist (his high point in this field came with his canonization of a Borgia). In order to secure the supreme office it had been necessary for Urban to become an equally skilled political contortionist too. Despite agreeing with what Galileo said, Urban also agreed with his political advisors (who said the opposite). Much to Galileo's disappointment, he was not absolved from his vow of universal silence. But having made this clear, Urban then made a further stipulation which appeared to contradict this judgement – ending with some philosophical ruminations which seemed to reinstate the status quo (or not). In brief, Urban gave Galileo permission to write about 'the systems of the world', but only on condition that he didn't favour the Copernican over the Ptolemaic system. He ended on a profound, but somewhat ambiguous note: 'We can never know how God made the world, for God could have brought about precisely the same effects by ways quite unimaginable to man. Therefore we must not stick to one way of saying how the world is made, as this limits God's omnipotence.' Such a credo may have given Urban himself license to believe as many contradictory theories as his mind could embrace, but its underlying commandment was clear. Thou shalt not preach Copernicanism. In order to make this *crystal* clear, Galileo also received a rather less philosophical missive from the Cardinal Niccolo Riccardi, the Chief Censor.

Galileo returned to his villa outside Florence. Here he decided to take the pope at his word (whatever that might have been). For the next few years he devoted himself to writing 'Dialogue Concerning the Two Chief World Systems, the Ptolemaic and the Copernican' (*Dialogo Sopra i Due Massimi Systemi del Mondo, Tolemaico e Copernicano*). This is couched in the form of a dialogue between three main characters, which takes place over four days and is set in a pink palace in Venice. The location is recognizable as the palazzo of Galileo's friend Sagredo, who had died 12 years previously. This was to be Galileo's tribute to his great pal, and the many evenings they had spent together discussing science, literature and philosophy over fine wine (and whatever else lay beside them). Sagredo himself appears in the *Dialogue* – as the witty intellectual who tears into the ideas put forward by the rather disingenuously named Simplicio, who represents the Ptolemaic-Aristotelian point of view. Simplicio is rescued from this ridicule by the character Salviati, who attempts a wise reconciliation between the two opposing views. For example:

SAGREDO (growing tired of Simplicio's insistence on Aristotle's unfailing correctness): You are like a rich gentleman who has built and furnished a magnificent palace, only to discover its foundations are faulty. In order to save its treasures you resort to all kinds of ingenious props and buttresses.

SIMPLICIO: Please, do not refer so disrespectfully to Aristotle. He was the originator of logic, as well as being its finest exponent. It would be better if you first tried to understand him, before trying to refute him.

SALVIATI: Logic is the organ with which we philosophize. A craftsman may excel in making organs, but he doesn't necessarily know how to play one properly.

Salviati is allowed sufficient ambiguity for him to appear neutral, but it's pretty obvious which side he really supports.

The *Dialogue* was duly published in 1632, having been scrutinized and given the papal imprimatur by the Vatican Censor. The book was immediately greeted with acclaim in intellectual circles throughout Europe. Here was a masterpiece which straddled all fields. Not only was it a revolutionary work of science, but it was also profoundly philosophical and a literary masterpiece. Urban welcomed this reflected glory: the *Dialogue* was nothing more than the very work which he himself had suggested Galileo should write.

However, it was soon pointed out to the pope that Galileo's new treatise was far from being the unbiased work it was supposed to be. Simplicio may have (allegedly) been named after a celebrated ancient Greek commentator on Aristotle, but he was in fact made to live up to his name. According to the Jesuits – who had it in for Galileo for denigrating their intellectual mentor – Galileo's *Dialogue* was liable to do more damage to the Catholic Church, and more for the Protestant cause, 'than Luther and Calvin put together'.

The Pope was furious, and ordered the immediate prosecution of Galileo. Unfortunately, the Pope had to be informed that this just wasn't possible – for the simple reason that the book had been licensed by the papal authorities. Here for once was a situation where he couldn't have it both ways. The Pope was even more furious.

But the Jesuits were not so easily baulked, and soon found a way around this seemingly insurmountable obstacle. An incriminating document was now discovered in the papal archives. This showed that way back in 1616, during his audience with the chief papal theologian Cardinal Bellarmine, Galileo had specifically promised that he would stop 'teaching or discussing Copernicanism in any shape or form'. This meant that Galileo had 'extorted' the license for the *Dialogue* from the papal authorities. An immediate order went out for the prosecution of Galileo on 'vehement suspicion of heresy'.

Galileo realized that he was in real trouble. His

enemies had at last got their act together. He was in danger of becoming the scapegoat for everything that had gone wrong with the Church. (A much-needed role which had remained unfilled for far too long, in the opinion of many.)

Public stooge *numero uno* was not an enviable position, especially with the Inquisition hovering in the wings. It was only 30 years since the philosopher and scientist Giordano Bruno, who had also been known throughout Europe, had appeared before the Inquisition in Rome. And he had ended up burnt at the stake, his mouth stuffed with a gag so that he couldn't pass on his heresies, even at his moment of extremity.

When the inevitable summons to appear in Rome arrived at Galileo's villa outside Florence, he immediately claimed that he was too old and too ill to travel. As it happened, this was not much of an exaggeration. Galileo was by now 68 years old, and his health had begun to deteriorate. But this was not good enough. Galileo had been sent an invitation which he could not refuse.

To his surprise, Galileo found the Inquisition remarkably sympathetic. Instead of the usual subterranean cell, and attendant neolithic jailor,

Galileo was put up in some style (the manner to which he had by now become accustomed). Galileo decided that his best course was to stick to the truth. He immediately denied ever having signed a promise, such as that in the newly 'discovered' document. The Inquisition, who had drawn their own conclusions about this document, decided that a discreet compromise was in order. Surely a form of words could be worked out, so that the venerable old man could be sent on his way with a reprimand? But others felt differently. Galileo had to be made an example of – or the Church would become a laughing stock.

Pope Urban VIII was already beginning to suspect that things were getting out of hand. After all, some of the finest minds throughout Europe believed what Galileo had said. (Perhaps he even had himself – though he couldn't be too sure on this point.) Urban remained in two minds. But the Jesuits knew how to tip the balance. They informed Urban that in the *Dialogue* the laughable character of Simplicio had been based on none other than himself!

Galileo was duly sentenced – to an unspecified term of imprisonment. But first, it was decided that he must be made to deny his Copernicanism. Galileo soon broke down under interrogation. (In Brecht's play *Galileo* he is simply led to the door of the torture chamber and shown the instruments. This scene never took place, but has a certain poetic correctness.) Galileo abjectly recanted his heretical science. He was made to swear that he 'abjured, cursed and detested' his heliocentric views – though according to legend, he couldn't help muttering under his breath: 'But it still moves.'

Galileo knew that what he had sworn was false. And he knew that his admirers would realize he had let them, and science, down. A broken man, he had not been made of the stuff of martyrs. Was he a coward, or simply prudent? The question remains open to this day. It is not a simple question, and any answer must take into account the psychology of this proud, bombastic, but deeply flawed and inwardly uncertain man – as well as his lifelong devotion to the cause of science, and understanding of all it stood for. Perhaps it is kinder just to say that he was wise.

In the event, Galileo's prison sentence was revoked by the Pope. Instead he was sent home, and forbidden to leave his villa outside Florence. For the last eight years of his life Galileo lived under virtual house arrest. Despite his age, and ailing health, he continued to pursue his scientific researches. As late as 1637, just months before he became completely blind, he discovered with his telescope that the moon wobbled on its axis. But his most important work of this period was his *Discourse Concerning Two New Sciences*. This too was couched in the form of a dialogue between his beloved Sagredo, the wise Salviati, and the hapless Simplicio. In this work Galileo summed up many of his thoughts on mechanics, and set down results drawn from a lifetime of experiments. The manuscript was smuggled out of Italy by the French ambassador to Rome, the Comte de Noailles, on his return to Paris. By now the students from France and Holland, England and Germany, whom Galileo had taught at Padua, had become professors at the universities in their native lands. It was they who acclaimed Galileo's work when it was finally published in Holland, and passed on copies of it to their students. The scientific revolution had begun, and was now unstoppable.

Galileo eventually died, infirm and blind – but

famous throughout Europe, just as he had always wished – on January 8th 1642. Later in the same year, Newton was born in England. Three hundred and fifty years later, in 1992, the Vatican finally saw its way to admitting that in the case of Galileo 'errors were made'.

CHRONOLOGY OF GALILEO'S LIFE

1564	Born at Pisa
1581	Enters University of Pisa to study medicine
1585	Leaves Pisa without degree to live with family in Florence. Starts teaching and tutoring
1589	Secures appointment as Professor of Mathematics at University of Pisa
1590–1	Writes *De Motu*
1592	Secures prestigous post as professor of mathematics at University of Padua
1609	Newly invented telescope arrives in Italy, and is developed by Galileo
1610	Publishes *The Starry Messenger* with great success. Moves from Padua to Florence under patronage of Grand Duke Cosimo II

1611	Demonstrates his new telescope in Rome
1614	Publicly attacked by Church
1616	Forbidden to 'hold or defend' the Copernican system by the Church
1623	Publishes *The Assayer*. Maffeo Barberini becomes Pope Urban VIII and gives Galileo permission to write a book about the two rival cosmologies
1632	After eight years work publishes *Dialogue Concerning the Two Chief World Systems*. Church summons Galileo to Rome
1633	Trial by the Inquisition results in sentence of life imprisonment. Renounces 'heretical science'. Lives under virtual house arrest outside Florence for the rest of his life
1638	Manuscript of *Discourses and Mathematical Demonstrations concerning Two New Sciences* smuggled to Holland where it is published
1639	Becomes completely blind
1642	Dies aged 77

SUGGESTIONS FOR FURTHER READING

James Reston Jnr: *Galileo* (Cassel) – Most readable and informative of the more recent popular biographies.

Pietro Redondi: *Galileo: Heretic* (Lane, Penguin) – Concentrates on the trial and its background, including information from recently unearthed documents in the Vatican archives.

Galileo Galilei (trs. Stillman Drake, introduction Albert Einstein): *Dialogue Concerning the Two Chief World Systems* – The maestro's work, introduced by the 20th century master.

Ernan McMullin (ed): *Galileo: Man of Science* (Basic Books) – Wide range of essays covering aspects of the man, his work, his influence. Expert, without being too scholarly.